Myths and Civilization of the

ANCIENT ROMANS

This edition first published in 1999 by
Franklin Watts
96 Leonard Street
London EC2A 4XD

Franklin Watts Australia
14 Mars Road
Lane Cove
NSW 2066

ISBN 0 7496 3643 2

The Myths & Civilization series
was created and produced by McRae Books,
via de' Rustici, 5 – Florence, Italy

Editors Anne McRae, Ronne Randall
Illustrations Francesca D'Ottavi (myths),
Ivan Stalio, Alessandro Cantucci, Andrea Morandi,
Fabiano Fabbrucci, Sauro Giampaia (civilization)
Graphic Design Marco Nardi
Cutouts Adriano Nardi, Ornella Fassio
Colour separations Litocolor., Florence (Italy)

Printed in Italy by Grafiche Editoriali Padane, Cremona

00 99 98   1   2   3   4
First edition

Myths and Civilization of the

ANCIENT ROMANS

John Malam

Illustrations by
Francesca D'Ottavi
Studio Stalio

W
FRANKLIN WATTS
NEW YORK • LONDON • SYDNEY

CONTENTS

INTRODUCTION

The civilization of the Romans spanned more than 1,000 years. From modest beginnings in a region of northern Italy, the Empire of the Romans spread out to cover many parts of Europe, North Africa and the Middle East. Within this vast area lived millions of people who came under Roman rule. Some had been conquered in battle by the Roman army; others had accepted the Romans without a struggle. The Romans spread their culture far and wide. Roman coins made in Britain or France could be spent in Spain and Greece, Israel and Egypt. The Roman language, Latin, became the first international tongue – just as English is today. It was in Latin that the myths of the Romans were first spoken and written, telling tales about the history of the Roman people and of Rome – the city which was the heart and soul of the Roman world.

HOW THIS BOOK WORKS

This book is divided into sections. Each section starts with a Roman myth, strikingly illustrated on a black background. After each myth comes a double-page information section which looks at an aspect of Roman culture and society, such as daily life, religion or the army.

The myth about the twins Romulus and Remus, and how Romulus built a fine city, leads into a non-fiction section about the city of Rome.

A myth is a story. It can be about the gods and their powers, the adventures of heroes, fabulous beasts or strange places where mortal humans cannot go. In the ancient world, the Mesopotamians, Egyptians and Greeks all told stories like these. The Romans told myths too – but most were not like the myths told in other lands. This was because many Roman myths told stories about ordinary people. The Romans believed their myths told them about themselves, especially about their own history. In this book we explore Roman mythology and civilization. By combining the two, we show how a knowledge of Roman myths provides a basis for understanding Roman society.

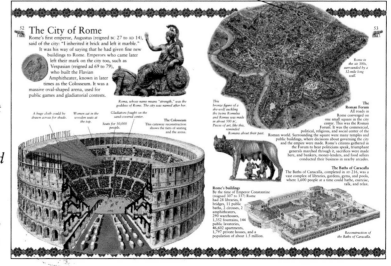

AENEAS, THE FATHER OF THE ROMANS

Long ago, the citizens of Rome told a story about a warrior from the east who came to live in the land of the Romans. His name was Aeneas, and to them he was the father of the Romans.

The story of Aeneas begins when the goddess Aphrodite came to Earth. She visited Phrygia, that part of the world where Turkey is now, and where the city of Troy once stood. Aphrodite walked among the human race and fell in love with Anchises, King of Troy.

She bore him a son, whom they called Aeneas. The young Aeneas was cared for by nymphs, but when he was five years old Aphrodite took him away and gave him to his father. Overcome with joy, Anchises boasted that Aphrodite was the mother of his son. On hearing this, Zeus, the ruler of all gods, grew angry. He threw a thunderbolt at Anchises, striking him on the leg and making him lame.

There came a time of war, when soldiers from Greek cities attacked Troy. After ten years of fighting, Troy fell to the Greeks. They invaded the city and set it on fire. Aeneas knew this was the end – there was nothing he could do to save the city. Carrying his aged father on his back, and his young son in his arms, Aeneas escaped to the safety of nearby mountains. For many months they lived there with other survivors from Troy. They built ships, and when the time was right Aeneas led his fellow Trojans in search of a new home.

From Phrygia, Aeneas set sail with a fleet of twenty ships. He stopped at many islands, and on one a fortune-teller made a strange prediction. He told Aeneas he would be at home only when he was so hungry he ate the plate his food came on.

After a long voyage, Aeneas and his ships reached Sicily. But for old Anchises the journey ended there. He died and was buried on the island. The final part of Aeneas's travels took him to Italy, where on the banks of the River Tiber he shared a meal with the rest of the Trojans. Such was their hunger that they ate the thin loaves of bread they were using as plates. The prediction had come true, and Aeneas knew he was home at last.

Aeneas was in the region known as Latium, the homeland of the Latins. He married the daughter of their king so that the Trojans and Latins were united as one people. Centuries later, when the city of Rome was founded in Latium, its citizens traced their family trees back to Aeneas the Trojan.

Origins

Italy is a country in the south of
Europe. It is a peninsula, which
means it is almost completely
surrounded by sea. About 2,500
years ago, groups of people settled
here. One group built their villages on
a fertile plain along the west coast of central
Italy. They were the Latins, whose cluster of
hilltop villages grew into the city of Rome.
In later years the Romans told a story about
the founding of Rome in which they said the
city began in 753 BC. Rome became the greatest
city of the ancient world, ruling an empire
which spanned Europe and reached as far as
the Middle East and Africa.

*The Villanovans lived in
northern Italy before the Romans. They
made metal objects, such as this incense
burner.*

The Etruscans

The Etruscans settled in the region of
Etruria (modern Tuscany and
Umbria) in about 800 BC. They were
cultured, civilized people and the
Romans learnt much from them. The
alphabet came to the Romans from
the Etruscans, as did gladiator fights,
chariot races and some gods. For a
time they were the most powerful
people in central Italy, but from
about 500 BC their power gradually
slipped away.

The birth of the city of Rome
Rome began as a village of huts, built
on top of a hill. The hill, which later
became known as the Palatine Hill,
was one of several hills close to the
River Tiber. The first huts, belonging to
farmers and shepherds, appeared on the
Palatine Hill around 1000 BC. Other
villages were built on the nearby hills. By
about 750 BC the villages had joined
together to make a town, and
this marked the birth of Rome.

*Etruscan warriors wore
helmets with high crests,
and carried javelins and
round shields.*

*The coast of North
Africa, where Tunisia is
today, was the home of
the Carthaginians. They
were seafaring traders,
who clashed with both
the Greeks and the
Romans. Their
capital was Carthage.*

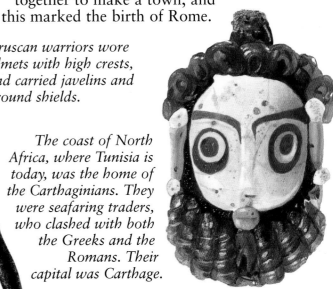

From monarchy to republic

Rome was at the center of a region called Latium. The inhabitants of the region were the Latins. To the north were the Etruscans, who took control of Rome and ruled there for 100 years. Under the Etruscans, Rome was ruled by kings. The town grew into a city, but the Latins were unhappy at being ruled by cruel "foreign" kings. In 510 BC, the Latins rebelled and threw the Etruscans out. From then on, Rome was a republic, ruled by a group of its leading citizens.

The chariot and goddess Roma on these silver coins celebrated the city of Rome.

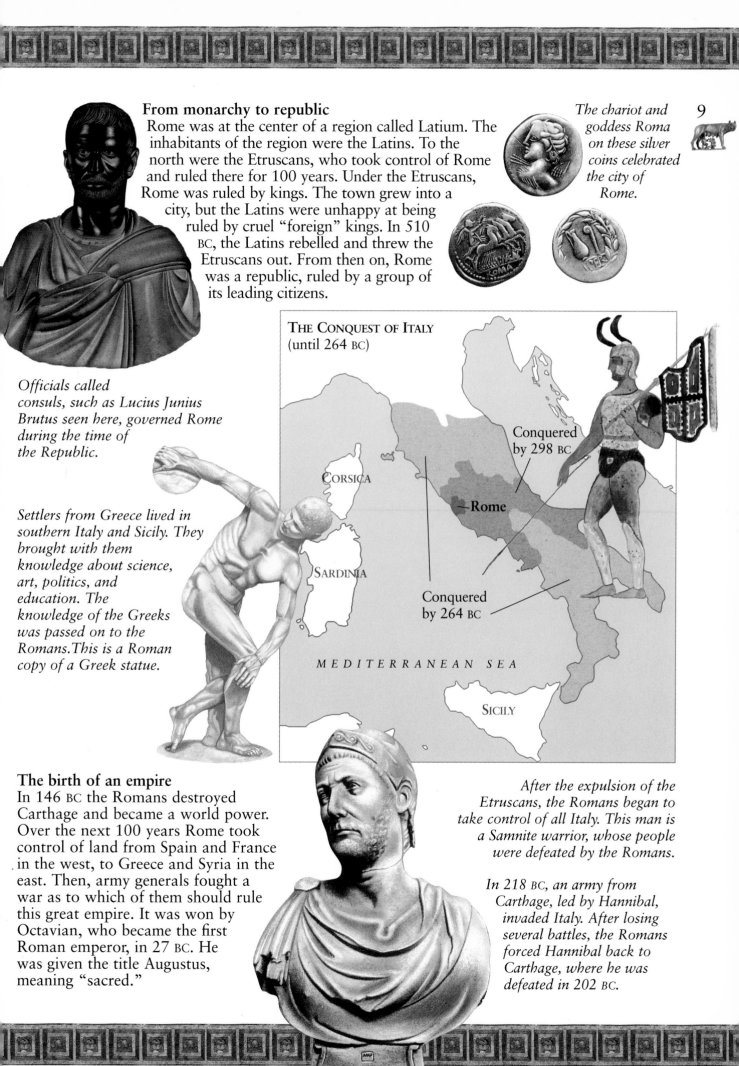

Officials called consuls, such as Lucius Junius Brutus seen here, governed Rome during the time of the Republic.

Settlers from Greece lived in southern Italy and Sicily. They brought with them knowledge about science, art, politics, and education. The knowledge of the Greeks was passed on to the Romans. This is a Roman copy of a Greek statue.

THE CONQUEST OF ITALY
(until 264 BC)

CORSICA

SARDINIA

Conquered by 298 BC

Rome

Conquered by 264 BC

MEDITERRANEAN SEA

SICILY

The birth of an empire

In 146 BC the Romans destroyed Carthage and became a world power. Over the next 100 years Rome took control of land from Spain and France in the west, to Greece and Syria in the east. Then, army generals fought a war as to which of them should rule this great empire. It was won by Octavian, who became the first Roman emperor, in 27 BC. He was given the title Augustus, meaning "sacred."

After the expulsion of the Etruscans, the Romans began to take control of all Italy. This man is a Samnite warrior, whose people were defeated by the Romans.

In 218 BC, an army from Carthage, led by Hannibal, invaded Italy. After losing several battles, the Romans forced Hannibal back to Carthage, where he was defeated in 202 BC.

THE WOLF AND THE TWINS

Rome was a wonder to behold, the greatest city the world had ever known. A million people lived there – Romans, foreigners and slaves. Within its walls were seven hills, the most important of which was the Palatine Hill. The Romans believed that this hill was where the city of Rome had begun.

A long time before Rome's first building stones were laid, there lived a cruel and unkind man called Amulius. His older brother, Numitor, was the king of a city in Latium. After a violent struggle, Amulius overthrew Numitor and made himself king. Then he turned on Numitor's family, killing his sons and forbidding his daughter, Rhea Silvia, from having children. Amulius did these terrible things to prevent Numitor from having descendants who might one day seek their revenge. Amulius was sure his plan would succeed. But when Rhea Silvia gave birth to twin boys, whose father was the god Mars, Amulius ordered that they should be drowned in the River Tiber. His servants took the babies, whose names were Romulus and Remus, and placed them in a basket. But they were too kind-hearted to carry out Amulius's orders, and so they left the basket to float away to safety.

It came to rest beside a fig tree, where it was found by a she-wolf who had heard the babies' cries. She fed them with her own milk and a woodpecker gave them scraps of food. When a shepherd saw this he knew at once who the babies were. He took them home to his wife and they raised them as their own sons.

Romulus and Remus grew into fine young men. One day the shepherd met Numitor and told him that his grandsons were alive and well. When Romulus and Remus learnt who they really were, they sought revenge against Amulius. He was killed, and Numitor was king once more.

The brothers now decided to build a city of their own. They chose a place on the banks of the River Tiber, close to where they had been left to die as infants. But they quarrelled as to who should name the city and become its king. Since they did not know which twin was the elder, they left it to the gods to send a sign. They stood on separate hills, and looked to the heavens. Remus saw six vultures, but Romulus saw twelve. Each believed the gods had meant him to be king – Remus because he saw the birds first, Romulus because he had seen the most.

A fight began and Romulus killed his brother. By himself Romulus built the city on the hill which the Romans later called the Palatine Hill. He named the city Rome, after himself.

The City of Rome

Rome's first emperor, Augustus (reigned 27 BC – AD 14), said of the city: 'I inherited it brick and left it marble.' It was his way of saying that he had given fine new buildings to Rome. Emperors who came later left their mark on the city too, such as Vespasian (reigned AD 69 – 79), who built the Flavian Amphitheatre, known in later times as the Colosseum. It was a massive oval-shaped arena, used for public games and gladiatorial contests.

Roma, whose name means 'strength', was the goddess of Rome. The city had many statues of her.

A huge cloth could be drawn across for shade.

Women sat in the wooden seats at the top.

Gladiators fought in the sand-covered central arena.

Seats for 50,000 people.

RECONSTRUCTION OF THE COLOSSEUM

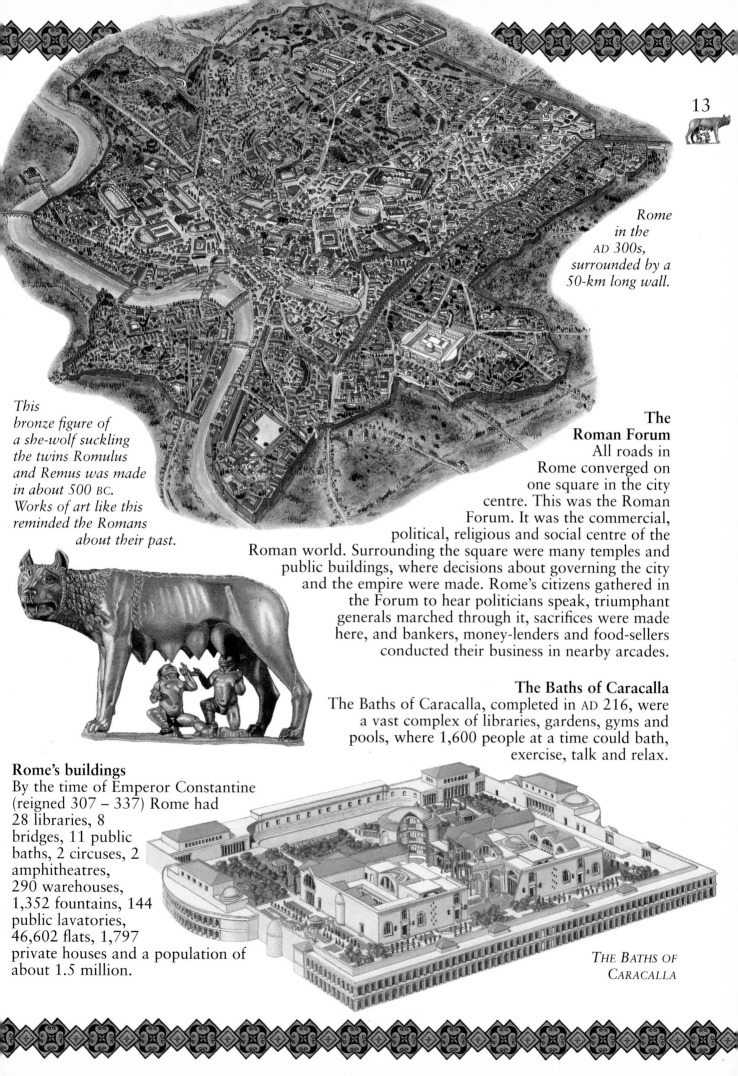

Rome in the AD 300s, surrounded by a 50-km long wall.

This bronze figure of a she-wolf suckling the twins Romulus and Remus was made in about 500 BC. Works of art like this reminded the Romans about their past.

The Roman Forum

All roads in Rome converged on one square in the city centre. This was the Roman Forum. It was the commercial, political, religious and social centre of the Roman world. Surrounding the square were many temples and public buildings, where decisions about governing the city and the empire were made. Rome's citizens gathered in the Forum to hear politicians speak, triumphant generals marched through it, sacrifices were made here, and bankers, money-lenders and food-sellers conducted their business in nearby arcades.

The Baths of Caracalla

The Baths of Caracalla, completed in AD 216, were a vast complex of libraries, gardens, gyms and pools, where 1,600 people at a time could bath, exercise, talk and relax.

Rome's buildings

By the time of Emperor Constantine (reigned 307 – 337) Rome had 28 libraries, 8 bridges, 11 public baths, 2 circuses, 2 amphitheatres, 290 warehouses, 1,352 fountains, 144 public lavatories, 46,602 flats, 1,797 private houses and a population of about 1.5 million.

THE BATHS OF CARACALLA

CLAUDIA AND THE GREAT MOTHER

In 204 BC Rome was at war with Carthage, a city on the north coast of Africa. The Carthaginian army had invaded Italy and the Romans were desperate to find a way to drive the foreigners from their land.

Rome's leaders consulted the Sibylline Books – a collection of prophecies. They guided the Romans in times of trouble, and in the war with Carthage a prophecy told them how to defeat their enemy. It said: 'The mother is absent. You must find her. When she comes, she must be received by honest hands.'

The Romans were puzzled, and a group of them went to the oracle, or fortune-teller, at Delphi, in Greece, for more information. There they were told to: 'Fetch the Great Mother who lives on Mount Ida.'

Now they knew what they must do to save Rome, for they knew that the Great Mother was none other than the goddess Cybele, the mother of the gods. Her symbol on Earth was a sacred stone, and just as the oracle had said, it was on Mount Ida, in the land of Phrygia. The Romans had to take the stone to Rome.

With the stone on board their ship, the Romans sailed back to Rome. But as their journey neared its end, disaster struck. As the ship entered the mouth of the River Tiber it became stuck on a sandbank.

Strong men pulled on ropes tied to the ship, but it would not move. People grew worried that the goddess Cybele was unhappy. Perhaps this was an omen that Rome would lose the war. Then a woman called Claudia Quinta, who had been wrongly accused of a crime she had not committed, prayed to Cybele. With arms held high, Claudia prayed that Cybele would send a sign to prove she was innocent.

Then Claudia gently pulled on one of the ropes tied to the ship and, miraculously, it moved as easily as if it were a toy. This sign from heaven proved Claudia's innocence. Freed from the sandbank, the ship sailed into port.

Just as the prophecy had foretold, the Great Mother had been received by honest hands, and now that the sacred stone was in Rome, the Romans knew they would soon win the war.

Religion

Roman religion grew from an ancient belief in spirits. It was the spirits who guided people's lives. As time passed, the spirits became the gods and goddesses of the Romans. Each one had special powers. In some parts of the Roman world people believed in other gods. When the religion of the Christians, who believed in only one true God, reached Rome, it spread quickly and replaced the gods of old.

Chief god of the Romans was Jupiter. He was god of sky, daylight and weather.

Some temples grew into large complexes, with courtyards surrounded by colonnades.

Roman temples
A temple was a house for a god. Inside was a statue of the god. Worshippers believed the god lived within the statue. It faced the door so it could 'see' the courtyard outside.
At an altar in the courtyard, sheep were sacrificed and gifts were left to please the god.

Bacchus was the god of wine. His followers held wild, drunken parties, dancing and calling out to him.

Sabazius was a god of creation from the east. His sign, a raised hand, was adopted by early Christians in Rome.

Superstition
Superstition played a great part in the lives of many Romans. Astrologers studied the stars to predict the future. Sorceresses – who were like witches – mixed potions to bring good luck or bad luck. Ordinary people wrote curses to harm others, and there was widespread belief in ghosts and evil. It was bad luck to fall over in the street or to hear an owl hoot – but it was good luck to see bees and snakes.

RECONSTRUCTION OF THE TEMPLE OF FORTUNA PRENESTINA, NEAR ROME.

After AD 313, Christians could openly worship their God. At first they met in houses, but soon churches were built, like this one.

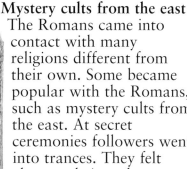

Peter and Paul were Christians who took Christianity to the Romans. Both were executed in Rome.

Mystery cults from the east

The Romans came into contact with many religions different from their own. Some became popular with the Romans, such as mystery cults from the east. At secret ceremonies followers went into trances. They felt close to their god.

Isis, a goddess from Egypt, was worshipped by some Romans. Followers of her cult believed in life after death. In their ceremonies they sang hymns, read from sacred books and shook rattles.

Christianity

Christianity was an eastern religion which came to Rome in the AD 40s. Unlike the Roman religion which had many gods, Christians worshipped only one God. They believed they were favoured people, blessed with the promise of eternal life. For almost 300 years the Romans persecuted the Christians, who were forced to meet in secret.

By spilling the blood of a bull, the eastern god Mithras gave life to all living things.

Religion in the home

In their daily lives the Romans believed they were constantly watched over by spirits. Some spirits, called lares, protected the home. At the start of each new day the family said prayers at the household shrine, or lararium, like the one seen here. Small gifts of food were left at the shrine, to please the spirits and ask for their protection.

GREEK GODS INTO ROMAN GODS

The Romans learnt many things from their neighbours, the Greeks. The Greeks had gods whom they believed controlled both nature and people's lives. The Romans adopted many of these gods and worshipped them as their own. They gave them Roman names. For example, Zeus, the chief Greek god, became Jupiter, and Hera, his wife, became Juno.

THE SACRED FIRE OF ROME

Long before Rome became a great city, it was a small hill village. Inside each crudely built house was a hearth where a fire burned. There was no chimney, and smoke was left to find its way out through gaps in the walls and roof. Fires were kept permanently alight in people's homes as an act of worship to the gods: a cold hearth meant an empty, godless house. Rome's first fire, said the Romans, had been lit from a spark brought by Aeneas from the faraway city of Troy. Aeneas, the father of the Romans, had carried the sacred fire of Troy across seas and mountains, and it was his gift to the people of Rome.

As the years passed, the village grew. There were other villages on nearby hills, and they grew too, until eventually they came together to make a town. From that town came the city of Rome.

Rome was a magnificent city. At its centre was the Forum, a large area surrounded by temples, arches, columns and statues. From one of the temples a plume of smoke drifted into the sky. This was the Temple of Vesta, built in honour of the goddess of the hearth. It was a small temple and, unlike the others, it was round. It was built that way to remind Romans of the first houses and the city's humble beginnings.

A fire was kept constantly alight inside the Temple of Vesta, just like the fires that had burned inside Rome's first houses. It was the sacred fire of Rome. If it died, Rome would be in danger.

Near the temple was the House of Vesta. It was the home of six priestesses called Vestal Virgins. They became priestesses while still children, between the ages of six and ten, and then served the temple for thirty years. Their main duty was to keep the temple fire burning day and night, never letting it go out. But there were occasions when storms raged and draughts blew the fire out. When this happened, the Vestals were accused of neglecting their duties, and they were flogged. Some, however, escaped this punishment by performing miracles.

Take, for example, the priestess Aemilia, who was accused of allowing the fire to die. As her accusers watched, she prayed to the goddess Vesta to send a sign to prove she was innocent of the crime. Aemilia ripped a piece of linen from her dress and threw it onto the fire's cold ashes. A wisp of grey smoke curled up from the cloth. Then, out of the smoke came fire. Rome's sacred fire burned brightly once more, the city was safe, and Aemilia was spared from punishment.

Emperor and State

During the Roman Empire the head of state was the emperor. He was the supreme ruler of the Roman world. As Rome's influence spread out from Italy, the Roman Empire was formed. It reached its greatest extent during the reign of Trajan (reigned AD 98 – 117), when as many as 50 million people lived within its many parts, called provinces. The Romans wanted to take their ideas about civilization to the edges of the world. In return, the provinces sent food, slaves and other goods to Rome.

Julius Caesar (lived 100 – 44 BC) became the most powerful man in Rome.

Citizens of Rome
Only men counted as Roman citizens – those born to Roman citizens (the freeborn), those freed from slavery (freedmen) and those granted citizenship by the state. Men in all parts of the Empire could be citizens of Rome. They were protected by Roman law, and got state aid, such as free corn.

A statue showing the Vestal Virgins at their task of keeping Rome's sacred fire alight.

An eagle was the state's symbol of power.

EMPERORS AS DIVINE BEINGS
After Julius Caesar's murder in 44 BC, people began to think about him as if he were a god. This fact made a difference to the emperors who ruled the Roman Empire. Caesar's adopted son, Octavian, was the first Roman emperor (ruling as Augustus). Because Caesar was a god, therefore Augustus was the son of a god – and so most emperors were thought of as gods living on Earth for people to worship as divine beings.

An emperor's life
Marcus Aurelius (reigned AD 161 – 180), seen here on horseback, was thought of as the perfect emperor. He was a thoughtful man, devoted to his public duties to serve the people and protect the Empire. He kept a diary in which he wrote his thoughts about his life as emperor.

Augustus, the first Roman emperor

In 27 BC, Augustus became the first emperor, and the period known as the Roman Empire began. His reign was marked by peace, order and good government. It was a time when new buildings were built in Rome. Augustus himself was short, was married three times and had one child, a girl.

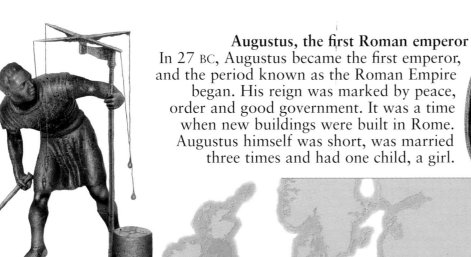

THE ROMAN EMPIRE
AT ITS GREATEST EXTENT

Roads led out from Rome across the Empire. They took the most direct routes, worked out by surveyors (above) who used a groma, to plot their straight lines.

BRITAIN

GAUL

ITALY

SPAIN

GREECE TURKEY

NORTH AFRICA

MEDITERRANEAN SEA

EGYPT

Feeding Rome's poor

In the mosaic above, a state official is handing grain to Rome's poorest citizens. The 'corn dole' prevented poverty and starvation, made work for people in the city's warehouses and ensured that the poor – about 200,000 in total – would support the government.

Even after 2,000 years, many fine examples of Roman architecture survive, such as this aqueduct in North Africa that carried drinking water to a city.

THE SLAVE GIRLS SAVE THE CITY

In 390 BC Rome was looted by the Gauls, who came from uncivilized lands to the north. The Gauls stayed in Rome for many months, and only left after they were given a large amount of gold.

With the barbarians gone, the Romans expected life to return to normal. But they were mistaken. Rome had been weakened by the Gauls, and after they left a second attack was made against the city.

This time, Rome was attacked by the Latins – the people in whose territory Rome was built. The army of the Latins camped outside Rome, and ambassadors were sent into the city with a message. It said: 'Send us your daughters to be our brides, for we wish the Latins and the Romans to be brought closer together.' When the message was read out, there was panic in the streets, and for a while no one knew what to do. Then a slave girl, whose name was Philotis, came forward. She had an idea.

Philotis said she and other young slave girls should go to the Latins and pretend to be freeborn Roman women. Then, at night, she would signal to the Romans that they could attack their enemy

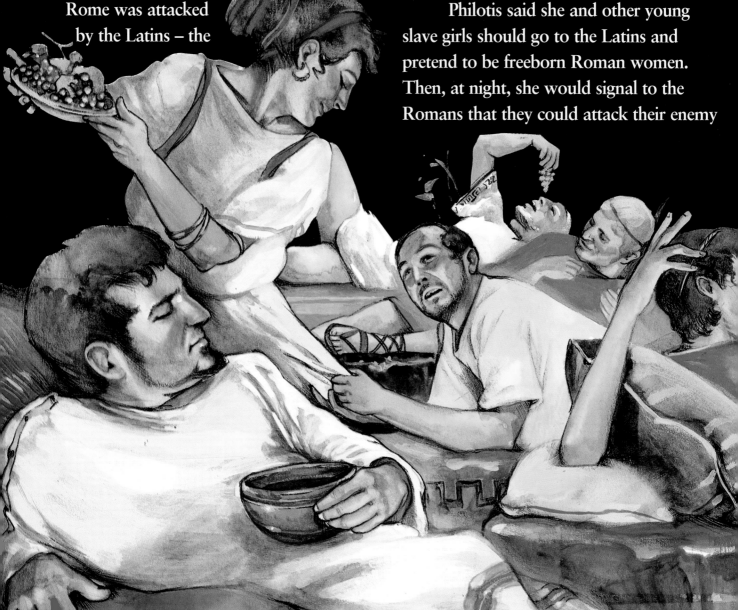

while they lay in their beds. The Romans listened as Philotis explained her plan. All agreed it was their only hope to save Rome from disaster.

Philotis and her fellow slave girls were given fine clothes and gold jewellery to wear, and dressed as brides they went into the camp of the Latins. Once inside they told the Latins that it was a special day for the Romans too. They said it was a festival day, when Romans drank, ate and enjoyed themselves. In the feast that followed, the slave girls served the Latins with food and drink. The Latins, who were soon drunk, fell into a deep sleep. While the girls hid the

Latins' swords, Philotis climbed a fig tree and waved a burning torch. This was the signal, and an army of Roman soldiers left Rome and headed towards the Latins' camp. Unseen, they crept into the camp and slaughtered the Latins as they slept.

Rome was safe, and every year thereafter, on 7 July, a feast was held to honour Philotis and the other girls. Called the 'Feast of the Fig Tree', it was a day when female servants were allowed to do as they pleased, and when Romans remembered how their city had been saved by the bravery of the slave girls.

Food, Feasts and Entertainment

Farmers were the backbone of Roman society. They grew the food that went to market to feed the people who lived in towns. It was in towns where life was lived to the full. Visitors from near and far came to be entertained, enjoying an afternoon watching a play in an open-air theatre, the thrills and spills of chariot racing or the drama of the games in the arena. And afterwards there might be a meal: a banquet in the house of a wealthy Roman or, for the poor, something cheap and simple in one of the town's many taverns.

In the arena gladiators fought with swords, spears and tridents. Some wore armour and helmets like this one.

A Roman marriage

The Romans had arranged marriages, where fathers chose husbands for their daughters. Marriage marked the passing of a girl to her husband. Her husband took charge of her from then on. At the ceremony, the bride, dressed in white, was aided by a matron of honour. The couple signed a contract, joined hands, and said their vows.

Chariots raced at a track called a 'circus'. The best horses came from Spain.

Skilled craftworkers

The Romans had many crafts. They made objects out of stone, clay, glass, metal, wood, bone, ivory and leather.

Glass vessels (left and below) were a luxury only the rich could afford. The poor used cheaper vessels made from pottery.

Public entertainment

When a town staged its games, people flocked to the local arena to watch gladiators fight each other or wild beasts. Elsewhere in town, charioteers raced at great speed around a race track, drawn by two, three or four horses, while at the theatre tragic or comic plays were staged.

At the theatre actors wore masks to show if they were sad or happy.

When the wheat harvest was gathered, the grains of corn were taken to a mill, like the one here. Water from a river or stream was channelled through to the mill, where it flowed over a water wheel. As the force of the falling water turned the wheel, it made power to turn grindstones. Grain was crushed between the stones, and flour was made.

Wheat was crushed to make flour.

Bakers used flour to make bread and pastries. Some people baked their own at home.

Flour was used for baking or mixed with water to make porridge. The best wheat made very white flour.

Food of the poor
The poor made do with puls, which was a thick, sticky porridge or gruel made from cereal grains. They drank cheap wine, diluted with water.

Figs were a popular fresh fruit, eaten at meals.

Grapes made wine, which everyone drank.

Olives gave oil for cooking. They were also eaten fresh or pickled.

Food of the rich
Wealthy Romans held lavish banquets. Guests lay on couches and ate with their fingers. A feast lasted several hours, starting with shellfish, snails and eggs, then roast meat, sauces and cabbage, and finishing with fruit, nuts and pastries. Wine and water were drunk with each course.

FESTIVALS
Festivals were held on many days throughout the Roman year. They were public holidays, when people enjoyed themselves and gave thanks to the gods. A lot of festivals were linked to the seasons and marked important dates in the farming year. For example, at the festival of Fordicidia (15 April), cattle were sacrificed to ensure good crops, and at the festival of Vestalia (9 June) stores were cleaned ready for the grain from the harvest.

THE BATTLE OF THE CHAMPIONS

In the early days of Rome, the nearby city of Alba Longa was its rival. It too wanted to be the region's leading city, and its people, the Albans, thought they should be the masters of Rome. But while the Romans and the Albans quarrelled, they both knew their real enemy was across the River Tiber in Etruria. This was where the Etruscans lived, an old and powerful people who had lived in Italy far longer than either the Romans or the Albans.

The Roman and Alban leaders knew that if their armies fought each other, both sides would be weakened. It would leave them open to attack from the Etruscans, who would surely be the winners. And so the Romans and the Albans decided on a plan to settle their differences.

Each side chose a set of identical triplets to fight for them. The three Horatius brothers would fight for Rome, and the Curatius brothers would represent the Albans. It would be the Battle of the Champions, the fight to end all fights.

Clad in armour and brandishing swords, the Roman three attacked the Alban triplets. Before long, the Albans were wounded, and two of the Romans lay dead. The third, whose name was Publius Horatius, fled from the battlefield.

Onlookers watched as the three Albans chased Horatius. But Horatius was cunning. He was not running away out of fear, but because he knew the Albans were injured and their wounds would slow them down. Sure enough, the wounded Albans chased Horatius at different speeds, and he was able to turn and kill them one by one.

Horatius was declared the champion of champions, and Rome was proclaimed the supreme city. In recognition of his great deed, Horatius was awarded the cloaks and swords of the fallen Albans.

In Rome, Horatius was greeted as a hero. But when his sister met him she burst into tears. Only then did Horatius discover that she had been engaged to one of the Albans he had killed. Overcome with rage, Horatius plunged his sword into her heart crying: 'So perish all Roman women who mourn a foe!'

By this terrible act, Horatius had taken the law into his own hands. He stood trial and was sentenced to death by hanging. But the Roman people could not bring themselves to execute their hero, and so Horatius, the man who had single-handedly defeated the Albans, was set free.

The Roman Army

The Romans faced many enemies. At first it was their neighbours in Italy, such as the Etruscans and Samnites. As Romans began to form their Empire, carved from other lands, wars were fought against foreign nations. The army built parts of the Empire by conquest. But later, the army's job changed to defending the Empire's frontiers. During the AD 400s, the frontiers were crossed by barbarian tribes. The Roman army tried to push them back, but in the end the barbarians were too strong for the Romans.

The only soldiers permanently stationed in Rome were the 10,000 men of the Praetorian Guard. Their job was to defend the city and the emperor.

A fort was a soldiers' village. Supplies and troops came in by road.

A soldier's short sword, called a 'gladius', and its scabbard. It was a slashing weapon.

A soldier's metal helmet protected the head and neck.

Roman forts – the outposts of empire
Forts were built throughout the Roman Empire. Some were temporary marching camps, surrounded by ditches and banks of earth. Others were permanent settlements protected by stone walls. Inside were barrack buildings where the soldiers slept and ate, bathhouses, toilet blocks, workshops, doctors' quarters, granaries and stables.

Forts could be protected by steep-sided ditches, iron spikes rammed into the ground and pointed wooden stakes.

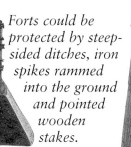

A siege tower with a battering ram was used to knock down an enemy's walls.

Organization of the army

During the Roman Empire, the army had about thirty large units called legions. Each legion had some 5,000 foot soldiers or legionaries, and a small number of horsemen. Legionaries were divided into ten groups called cohorts, with about 500 men in each. Cohorts were made up of small units, called centuries, with about 80 men in each. A century was under the command of a centurion.

Several types of heavy artillery machines were used to weaken an enemy. Catapults shot big arrows tipped with iron or burning rags, and other machines hurled heavy rocks over long distances.

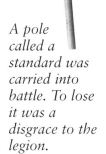

A pole called a standard was carried into battle. To lose it was a disgrace to the legion.

By raising shields above their heads, soldiers formed a 'testudo', or tortoise. It protected them from stones and arrows.

Battle tactics

Battles were usually planned long in advance. Scouts spied on an enemy and reported on their numbers and weapons. This gave the Roman generals time to decide the best way to mount an attack. Sometimes a town or stronghold was besieged. The army camped outside for weeks or months, waiting for the people inside to give in – or die of hunger.

Some of Rome's enemies fought with elephants, shooting arrows from towers on their backs.

THE RAPE OF LUCRETIA

In the days when Rome was ruled by an unpopular family of kings called the Tarquins, the Romans were at war with the nearby city of Ardea. One day, during a long siege, a Roman general called Collatinus fell into conversation with other commanders. They talked about their wives at home in Rome, and which of them was leading the most virtuous life.

Collatinus said that his wife, Lucretia, would win the contest. The others disagreed, and to solve the argument they rode to Rome to visit their wives by surprise. This way they would discover who was leading the most virtuous life.

The men went to their homes at night. All of the women, except one, were enjoying themselves at elegant dinner parties. Their husbands were shocked. But when Collatinus visited Lucretia, he found her at work with her maid-servants, spinning wool. She alone had lived up to everything her husband had claimed for her.

But Lucretia was more than just well-behaved. Men were struck by her great beauty, and one, Sextus Tarquinius, who had ridden to Rome with her husband, fell in love with her. He was a Tarquin, son of the king. A few days later Tarquinius returned secretly to Lucretia's house, where he was greeted as an honoured guest. He told Lucretia he had fallen in love with her. Lucretia would not hear of it. Tarquinius was determined to get his own way, and so he threatened to kill Lucretia and a slave. Lucretia was faced with a terrible choice: whether to give in to Tarquinius or die. Either way, her fate was sealed, and she gave in to the vile demands of Tarquinius.

After Tarquinius had left, Lucretia summoned her father and her husband. Each brought a friend. The four men listened to Lucretia's story. They did their best to comfort her, saying she should not feel guilty since it was Tarquinius who had forced himself upon her. Lucretia felt her honour had been taken from her. She picked up a knife and stabbed herself through the heart.

As for Tarquinius, he did not get away with his crime. When the people heard what he had done they rose up against the Tarquins and overthrew the monarchy. From then on Rome was a republic, no longer ruled by kings, but by men chosen by the people. For this, Lucretia was forever remembered by the Romans as the woman who gave them their freedom from tyrants.

Daily Life

Within a few minutes of waking up at dawn, Roman men and women were dressed and ready to begin the day. In wealthy families men went to the barber, while servants helped women to arrange their hair and jewellery. As the day progressed, there might be visits to the arena, theatre or the baths, before the evening meal at home, followed by bed for the night.

Roman mother and her servant bathing a child.

Emperor Septimus Severus (reigned AD 193 – 211), his wife Julia Domna, and their sons Geta and Caracalla. Geta, whose portrait is defaced, was murdered by Caracalla.

A woman gathering wild flowers. This scene was painted on the wall of a house.

Blocks of flats at Ostia housed Rome's growing population.

The importance of the family

Families were important in Roman society. To the Romans, the word *familia* meant a father, mother and their children, together with their slaves and close relatives. The father was the head of the family and the household. He set a good example for his sons to follow, since they would lead the family after his death.

Women in Roman society

It was a woman's duty to care for the family and the home, cooking, cleaning, looking after the children and making clothes. If she lived in a wealthy family, she ordered slaves to do the work. But women from poor families had to do this work on their own. Women could not vote, or work in the government.

Houses in towns and in the countryside

In Roman towns in Italy, the wealthy and their servants lived in private houses. They were single-storey buildings, with rooms built around a courtyard. Some had gardens. The poor lived in small, overcrowded flats built in blocks several storeys high. The dark rooms had no running water or toilets. In the countryside there were farms and villas, which were estates with a large house and several farms. Only the rich could afford villas, which they used as holiday homes, away from towns.

Women's hairstyles

Women took great care over their hair, which was always kept long. As fashions changed, different hairstyles were worn. The simplest style was for the hair to be drawn into a knot at the back of the head, where it was held in place with ribbons or pins. Ringlets, curls and plaits were also popular. Some women wore wigs, made with hair brought from Germany, or even from India. A mixture of vinegar and lentil oil was used to dye brown hair blonde.

In the AD 100s it was fashionable for women to wear their hair high at the front with a knot at the back.

Combs were made from ivory, boxwood and tortoiseshell. This one belonged to a woman called Modestina.

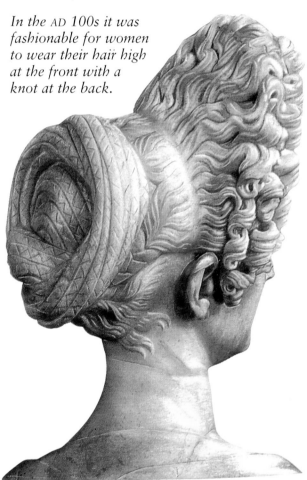

Necklace and ring made from gold and semi-precious stones.

Jewellery

The Romans wore necklaces, rings, chains, bangles and brooches. There were workshops in Rome, though much jewellery was made in the Middle East, at Alexandria and Antioch, by Greek jewellers. In the early years of Roman history pieces were made from plain gold, but as time went by jewellers added emeralds, sapphires, pearls and even diamonds to their creations.

Clothes and shoes

For much of Roman history the standard item of clothing for men was the toga. It was a large piece of semicircular woollen cloth, draped loosely from the shoulders. Women wore a long belted gown, called a stola. Both items went out of fashion during the time of the Roman Empire, replaced by simpler tunics decorated with wide stripes. Boots, sandals and indoor shoes were made of leather. Children wore the same styles as grown-ups.

QUEEN DIDO TRIES TO TRAP AENEAS

Many tales are told about Aeneas and the adventures he had as he sailed from Troy to Italy. Before Aeneas reached Italy, his ships were blown off course by a storm. Many of his faithful sailors were feared drowned. His seven remaining ships, their sails torn and timbers battered, headed to the shelter of an unfamiliar coastline. The coastline was that of North Africa, and Aeneas landed close to the city of Carthage, the home of Queen Dido. Aeneas ordered his crew to stay by their ships and set off towards the city. As he walked through the countryside, the goddess Venus appeared and told him about the people he would meet. To protect him, the goddess shrouded Aeneas in a mist which made him invisible.

Inside the city's great temple he watched as Queen Dido commanded her people to do her work. And then he saw something which amazed him, for standing in a group were the Trojan sailors he thought had drowned at sea. This was powerful magic indeed, and Queen Dido must surely be a great ruler to pluck men from the teeth of a storm. She listened as the Trojans told of their adventures with Aeneas, and how it was his plan to build a new city to replace Troy.

When Queen Dido said she must find Aeneas, the mist of invisibility that hid the hero from view suddenly lifted. Aeneas was revealed!

That night, at a banquet, Aeneas entertained the queen. She was captivated, not only by the stories she heard, but by Aeneas himself. She was soon in love with him, and began to plan a way of keeping him for herself.

But the gods had other plans for Aeneas, for they knew it was his destiny to sail to Italy. They watched as Queen Dido plotted to marry Aeneas and trap him in Carthage. Aeneas seemed unable to break free from her spell. The gods knew they must act, and they sent Mercury with a message.

Mercury, the god of travellers and messages, told Aeneas that his future lay in Italy, not with Queen Dido. When Aeneas, who was now free of her magic, told her he was leaving, she pleaded with him to stay. But it was no use. Aeneas knew he

must continue on his journey.

Overcome with grief, Queen Dido ordered a fire to be built. She wanted to destroy everything that reminded her of Aeneas. Then, as she watched the Trojans' ships depart, she fell on a sword and died. The fire was lit, and its flames consumed more than just the memories of Aeneas, for it was now Queen Dido's funeral pyre. As for Aeneas, he never looked back. He sailed to Italy and his future as the father of the Roman people.

Trade and Transport

The saying that all roads led to – and from – Rome is quite true. This was because the Golden Milestone in the city centre was the starting point for the Empire's roads. The names of towns and their distances from Rome were written on it in gold letters. Roads were not the only means of communication – the sea was just as important. Into Rome's ports came the wealth of her Empire – wines and fruits from Italy; corn and dates from North Africa; oil from Spain; meat, wood and wool from Gaul; marble from Greece; paper from Egypt – all to be sold in the city's markets.

Many a ship never reached its destination. Storms, pirates and rocks took their toll, sending sailors and ships to the seabed.

In towns, farmers and other traders sold their goods from market stalls, as in the scene shown here.

Bankers worked in the market-place, exchanging foreign currency and lending money.

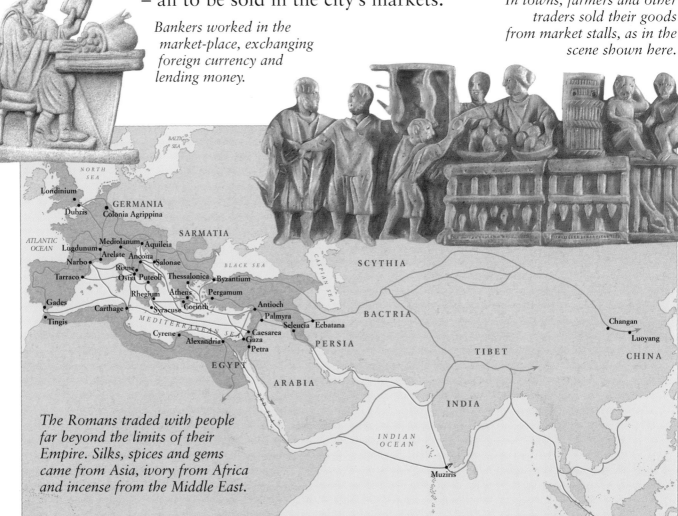

The Romans traded with people far beyond the limits of their Empire. Silks, spices and gems came from Asia, ivory from Africa and incense from the Middle East.

A network of roads

There were about 85,000 km of roads in the Roman world. Many were made by soldiers as the army extended the limits of the Empire. Later on, merchants, couriers and travellers used them.

THE MAIN ROADS
OF THE ROMAN EMPIRE

The postal system used couriers to carry letters across the Empire. They covered about 80 km a day.

The carving below shows a merchant ship sailing into Ostia, one of Rome's two main ports. To the right, customers at a city tavern enjoy wine from its cargo.

Merchant ships carrying grain and wild beasts from North Africa took two or three weeks to reach Rome.

Farmers and merchants used wagons to move their goods along the roads. Travellers went by horse or on foot. Some main roads had 'service stations' where horses could be fed and changed.

A balance for weighing goods. The weight is shaped like a person.

Coins and money

Mints – places where coins were made – existed in many towns in the Empire. The coins they struck could be used anywhere in the Roman world. They were made from bronze, silver and gold. Each type of coin had its own name and value.

Castor and Pollux – the Heavenly Twins

To the east of Italy is the land of Greece. The Greeks were very wise, and the Romans learnt many things from them. When the Romans learnt about Zeus and the other gods of the Greeks, they began to worship them as their own. The Romans gave them new names, so that the Greek god Zeus became the Roman god Jupiter.

The Greeks told stories about their gods. One story was about 'Zeus's boys' who were twin brothers called Castor and Polydeuces. The Romans called them Castor and Pollux, and, as time passed, they made up their own stories about the 'heavenly twins'.

The Romans told how Castor and Pollux helped them to win a battle against their neighbours, the Latins. Out of nowhere rode the twins. On white stallions at the head of the Roman cavalry, they charged at the Latins, who were soon defeated. Then, by some strange magic, the twins appeared in the centre of Rome, many miles from the battlefield. They watered their horses in a sacred pool, told the crowds about the Roman victory over the Latins and vanished.

In another story told by the Romans, Castor and Pollux were seen by a man called Publius Vatinius. He was on his way to Rome when he had a vision. It was late at night, and out of the darkness came the heavenly twins, riding along the road.

Their sudden appearance startled Vatinius. But he had nothing to fear, for the twins had good news, saying the Roman army had been victorious against their enemy, the Macedonians.

Vatinius hurried on to Rome and gave the news to the city's leaders. They did not believe him. They thought he was tricking them with lies – why would Castor and Pollux come to Vatinius and not them? Poor old Vatinius was taken away and locked up.

Many weeks later a messenger brought news that the Roman army really had defeated the Macedonians. At once, the people knew that Vatinius had told the truth – Castor and Pollux really had come to him just as he had said.

Vatinius was set free, and to make amends for the way he had been wronged he was given some land. As for Castor and Pollux, they continued to be worshipped by the Romans, in the temple built in their honour.

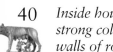
Inside houses, paintings in strong colours decorated the walls of rooms. Landscapes were popular, as were scenes from mythology.

Art, Literature and Science

The Romans were civilized, cultured people. Scientists, doctors and thinkers explored the world they knew, looking for ways to explain its many secrets. Artists recorded the world they saw in paintings, mosaics and sculptures. Books, poems and plays came from the pens of writers, and historians wrote about Rome's origins, emperors, wars and everyday life. It is from sources such as these that we are able to piece together the Roman world, bringing the past to life.

Pieces of coloured marble were used to make this mosaic picture of a tiger attacking a bull.

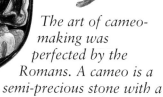

The art of cameo-making was perfected by the Romans. A cameo is a semi-precious stone with a design carved on it in relief. Cameos were used as jewellery (above left), and as inlays for furniture (above right).

BOOKS AND WRITING

The Romans wrote on papyrus, a type of paper made in Egypt from the stems of water reeds. Many small sheets of papyrus were joined together to make a long strip of paper. This was rolled around a wooden winding stick to make a book roll – the Roman version of a book. To write with, the Romans used pens made from the quills of birds' feathers or from pieces of bone. They were dipped into red or black ink. Mistakes could be rubbed out with a damp sponge. Large towns had libraries where many book rolls were kept.

Seneca *(about 5 BC – AD 65) was a writer, lawyer and philosopher. He wrote a book in which he poked fun at Emperor Claudius. Its English title is* The Pumpkinification of the Divine Claudius *– which was Seneca's way of saying the emperor was turning into a pumpkin!*

Ovid *(43 BC – AD 17) trained as a lawyer, but turned to poetry. His most famous work,* Metamorphoses, *is a collection of myths.*

Cicero *(106 – 43 BC) was a politician and writer. He studied law, Greek literature and oratory – the art of making speeches. Many of his speeches were written down, and they tell us about life in Rome.*

Virgil *(70 – 19 BC) is one of the greatest poets of the ancient world. His most famous work, the* Aeneid, *is the story of Aeneas, the father of the Roman people. It took 11 years to write.*

Mosaics

A mosaic is a pattern or a picture made from small pieces of coloured stone and glass, called *tesserae*. The Romans decorated the floors, walls and even ceilings of buildings with mosaics. The pieces were pressed into a bed of wet cement, which set hard. A mosaic surface was hard-wearing and long-lasting.

Pliny *(AD 23 – 79) was a scholar. As a young man he served in the army where he wrote about throwing missiles from horseback. His greatest work,* Natural History, *is an encyclopedia of popular science. He was killed watching the eruption of the volcano Vesuvius, in AD 79.*

Livy *(59 BC – AD 17) was a historian. His greatest work was a collection of 142 books, of which 35 have survived. They are the story of the city of Rome, from its very beginning to the year 9 BC.*

Doctors used more than 100 types of medical instrument (above) to operate on patients (right and far right).

Doctors and medicine

Roman doctors performed operations and prescribed medicines, many of which were based on herbal remedies. Garlic was mixed into potions used to treat leprosy, and saffron was used for eye complaints.

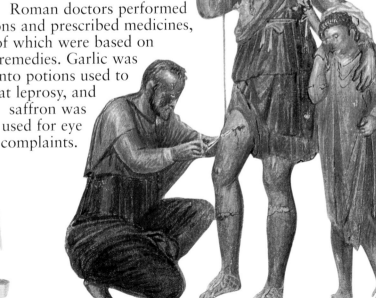

The Fall of the Western Empire

The vast Roman Empire was hard to control. In AD 284, Emperor Diocletian (reigned AD 284 –305) tried to make it easier to rule by splitting it in two – a western half and an eastern half, each with its own emperor. Some fifty years later the Emperor Constantine (reigned AD 307 – 337) chose a town in the east, in present-day Turkey, to be the new capital of the Roman world. He called it Constantinople. The Eastern Empire flourished, but the Western Empire collapsed. Barbarians invaded it and Rome was sacked. The end came in AD 476, with the resignation of the last emperor of the Western Empire.

Attila was a leader of the Huns, a tribe that originated in the east.

A Saxon warrior. Starting in the AD 500s, the Saxons spread from northern Europe into Britain.

Barbarian soldiers carried shields, swords and lances. They wore armour made from scale-like metal plates.

Justinian (reigned AD 527 – 565), the emperor of the Eastern Empire, reunited it with the Western Empire for about 20 years.

Statues like this show that the emperors of the Western and Eastern Empires had equal importance.

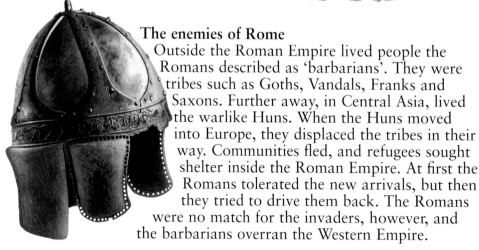

The enemies of Rome

Outside the Roman Empire lived people the Romans described as 'barbarians'. They were tribes such as Goths, Vandals, Franks and Saxons. Further away, in Central Asia, lived the warlike Huns. When the Huns moved into Europe, they displaced the tribes in their way. Communities fled, and refugees sought shelter inside the Roman Empire. At first the Romans tolerated the new arrivals, but then they tried to drive them back. The Romans were no match for the invaders, however, and the barbarians overran the Western Empire.

Trying to regain territory in the Middle East, Emperor Valerian (reigned AD 253 – 260) was taken prisoner by the Persian king, Shapur (right), and died a captive.

A Visigothic jeweller made this bronze and enamel brooch in the shape of an eagle.

Christianity survived the fall of the Western Empire, and the Church grew strong.

Londinium

Paris
Lugdunum
Burdigala · Mediolanum
Tolosa · Ravenna · Sirmium
Tarraco · Massilia Florentia
Rome
Caralis Neapolis
· Gades
Tingis · Carthage
Syracuse

Constantinople
Thessalonica
Athens
Corinthus · Ephesus
· Antioch

Leptis Magna Cyrene Alexandria
Jerusalem
Cairo

Vandals, Sueves
Huns
Ostrogoths
Visigoths
Franks
Angles, Saxons, Jutes
Lombards

The Byzantine Empire
Constantinople was a 'new Rome', in the east. It was the capital of the Byzantine Empire – another name for the eastern half of the Roman Empire. For 1,000 years it remained a major Christian city until, in 1453, it fell to the Muslims. It is now called

The great 6th-century church of Santa Sophia, Constantinople.

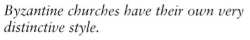

Byzantine churches have their own very distinctive style.

The legacy of the Romans
We have inherited much from the Romans. Some modern languages are influenced by Latin; some of our buildings are based on styles used by the Romans; we use roads planned by Roman engineers; and the Roman Catholic Church has its head-quarters in Rome – a link with Ancient Rome.

Theodora (right), Justinian's wife, was an able politician. She influenced many of her husband's decisions regarding the Empire.

A glass drinking horn (left) made by a Roman craftsman.